things I used to know

by

David W. Hamilton, Psy.D.

© 2013 David W Hamilton All Rights Reserved.

ISBN 978-1-304-19195-3

167hours.net/thingsIusedtoknow

Table of Contents

INTRODUCTION

When you are fighting your way through pain, hardship, or discouragement, your heart needs you to know some things.

ONE

So, you are ready to make the journey out of this? You are desperate to make the journey out of this?

TWO

Do you believe you are loved?

THREE

Ok, let's talk about some very practical things.

FOUR

Yes, you have losses,

FIVE

Everything that goes wrong, every irritation, gets a hotline right to your emotions.

SIX

I know you are tired.

SEVEN

I know that you look at the future and see obstacle after obstacle.

EIGHT

So how are you?

NINE

There are things you can imagine being different.

TEN

You have people who believe in you.

ELEVEN

There are some things, people, places, tasks, that you are avoiding.

TWELVE

Corners. Remember those?

THIRTEEN

It would be good if your everyday experiences came with "like" buttons.

FOURTEEN

Here's you…

FIFTEEN

Remember what I said about going through the motions?

SIXTEEN

When we go through hard times we stop doing things we used to enjoy, hobbies, past-times.

SEVENTEEN

> *You get mad at people.*

EIGHTEEN

> *Be careful of the balance between thinking and doing.*

NINETEEN

> *Sometimes the sadness hits so hard your stomach feels like it's been scooped out with a spoon.*

TWENTY

> *Where have all the people gone?*

TWENTY-ONE

> *"I can't do this!"*

TWENTY-TWO

> *Hope is believing that there is always another path to where you really need to go.*

TWENTY-THREE

> *Inside you are curled up in pain.*

TWENTY-FOUR

> *You've come to a dead stop?*

TWENTY-FIVE

> *You have stumbled and are still stumbling.*

TWENTY-SIX

You may have noticed by now that all is not smooth sailing on this trip.

TWENTY-SEVEN

I want you to stop what you're doing.

TWENTY-EIGHT

Memories pop up without a warning and with a will of their own.

TWENTY-NINE

Life goes on and there are things to celebrate.

THIRTY

You look for magic.

THIRTY-ONE

You slip and fall into a hole.

THIRTY-TWO

There are days when you don't think you can get out of bed.

THIRTY-THREE

Remember what I said about avoidance?

THIRTY-FOUR

I have given you thousands of words now but I am nowhere near done.

THIRTY-FIVE

Remember I told you before to trust the designer and trust the design?

THIRTY-SIX

You still lose heart and stand still.

THIRTY-SEVEN

You are turned inward.

THIRTY-EIGHT

You have now.

THIRTY-NINE

You were worried today, nervous, anxious, unsure, restless, apprehensive.

FORTY

You fear that you have made no progress at all, and even worse that you never will.

FORTY-ONE

I know your functioning has taken a hit in multiple areas of your life.

FORTY-TWO

You have those brief moments, or parts of the day, when the sunlight comes through the trees and shines on you.

FORTY-THREE

No matter how much of today has gone or how much you have messed it up, the rest of it still counts.

FORTY-FOUR

You want things to be better today, even pray for things to be better today.

FORTY-FIVE

You remember things from the past that are no longer in your life.

FORTY-SIX

See how they rise and fall, wax and wane, these emotions?

FORTY-SEVEN

Everywhere you look there are tasks you don't feel up to.

FORTY-EIGHT

You want to give up, cut yourself off.

FORTY-NINE

Fail! Fail! Fail! Again and again!

FIFTY

Right now stand up tall.

FIFTY-ONE

I have something I want you to do.

FIFTY-TWO

What did you like today?

FIFTY-THREE

They pass, those moments when you think you can't do it, think you shouldn't even try.

FIFTY-FOUR

Discouragement, low on courage.

FIFTY-FIVE

Get back up.

FIFTY-SIX

The day's not over.

FIFTY-SEVEN

It feels good, doesn't it?

FIFTY-EIGHT

Your vocabulary has had to include "I'm sorry" over and over.

FIFTY-NINE

You want things around you to change.

SIXTY

Sometimes you just want to run and never look back.

SIXTY-ONE

The wall of rock rises in front of you, cold, hard, intimidating.

SIXTY-TWO

That knot in your stomach again!

SIXTY-THREE

Sometimes you allow yourself to admit you have made a little progress or have moments when you feel a little better.

SIXTY-FOUR

You think you have made progress in acceptance,

SIXTY-FIVE

You have felt a level of pain that some are unaware of, that some cannot relate to.

SIXTY-SIX

Decision making, even a simple decision like what to do next, can be such a challenge that you coast to a halt.

SIXTY-SEVEN

The moments of sunshine, when all the barriers to light part just enough, and at the right time, to let a ray of light through, are you seeing those?

SIXTY-EIGHT

I think you are seeing now that there is more to life than these waves of hurt and sadness and fear. More, not less.

SIXTY-NINE

You are building on yesterday, today.

SEVENTY

There are things you can change.

SEVENTY-ONE

There are many ways to distance yourself from people you love.

SEVENTY-TWO

You have come so far and you keep trying day after day, and yet there are still times when you just don't feel like doing anything.

KEEP GOING

There is more to say and some of what I've said still needs to be heard over and over.

Introduction

When you are fighting your way through pain, hardship, or discouragement, your heart needs you to know some things.

If your heart could send you messages, what would they be? What is it that you used to know, but can't quite hold onto, in the clutter, confusion, or chaos of emotional pain?

As I start to write this book, or blog, or journal, whatever it will become, I am sitting in the parking lot outside an emergency room. About 2 years ago, on a Sunday afternoon, I followed an ambulance here. I talked to doctors and paced back and forth in the lobby. That night I came back to visit. I was the only one allowed in. It was late. The hospital seemed empty, lonely. I didn't stay long, sat next to the bed and didn't say much.

There are times when being present is all you have to give.

If I could do it again, I still wouldn't say much but I would stay longer. I found out later that even those few minutes left an impression that has not been forgotten.

I'm a psychologist. I believe in the healing power of being present with someone. I have always suspected that my best words to patients only help to make the presence tolerable, even reasonable, while the healing takes place.

So putting my words on these pages, as if they, disembodied, could encourage healing... is somewhat removed from what I do in my clinical work. But I write these words because the good things we know, the comforting truths we know, get pushed to the back of the shelf over time.

When there are injuries we need to recover from, wounds we need to see healed in our souls, we need those things we once knew. We need them to be close at hand.

We may have people present in our lives but we can lose access to the truths we know. It is like losing a part of ourselves, a vital part that we need to keep close.

We lose the comfort of our own presence.

So I write these words to help us all remember who we are, what we believe, and what we used to know.

If they are helpful for you, you are welcome to them. If I find they do not resonate with the hurting people I know, you will never read them.

David W. Hamilton, Psy.D.

Grand Rapids, Michigan

One

So, you are ready to make the journey out of this? You are desperate to make the journey out of this?

You have felt this before, the I-must-beat-this feeling. What will be different this time?

I will tell you.

This time I will not leave you to do it alone.[1] I will not forget you. I will not give up on you. I will remind you a hundred or a thousand times of things you would say you know, but have not been able to keep in your hands. I will keep picking them up when they clatter to the floor. I will pry open your fingers if I need to and give

---

[1] Did you read the introduction? Go ahead. I'll wait.

them to you again, and again, and again, until the clattering sound reminds you, not of something being lost, but of something being given and held.

You are tired, more than tired, worn, threadbare. You are afraid, at times even terrified. You are sad, hopeless, discouraged, lonely, angry, numb, guilty, ashamed.

All of those emotions and more have trudged by so often, with such heavy steps, that deep trenches, even ravines, have scarred your landscape and you despair of ever seeing the fields and meadows that are such a remote memory you wonder whose memories they are. The depth and length of your pain has broken you off from other people, the people who live in that other world, beyond the glass wall,

…where pain hurts but is bearable,

…where disappointment stings but goes away.

I know.

Here is what I remind you of today. People feel this way, the way you do. People have felt this way and people will continue to feel this way in the future. It is a human experience.

You are not as different as you feel.

The glass wall is not as thick and impenetrable as it seems.

You have sustained injuries. Your design allows you to withstand injury and suffer immense pain and still recover, to still be as human as anyone else that you see around you.

You have some knowledge of who designed you. Trust the designer and trust the design. I will have more to say about this again. I'm sure.

Two

Do you believe you are loved?

You know, don't you, that it is possible for a human to be deeply loved and not feel it?

…to hold a glass of water in your hands and not drink it,

…to have the answer staring you in the face and not see it.

Just because you don't see it does not mean it isn't there. Just because you are thirsty does not mean there is no water. Just because you do not feel loved does not mean you are unloved. Let me start a sentence for you to finish.

"If God really loved me..."

Ah! Things come to mind. Don't they?

You might not put it so bluntly but the echoes are there in your mind. You wonder why God has not rescued you, taken away the pain, provided something. As soon as you wonder, possible answers come flooding in. Maybe some of the answers comfort you but there are some that hurt or scare you.

Beware of the answer "I am not loved." "I don't matter." And even, "I am being punished." You say you believe in forgiveness. Do you? Yes, you have done some things that are wrong.

Ask God to search your heart.

Ask God for forgiveness.

Whatever God is doing or not doing, it is not because you are unloved. And hold on for this one... It is exactly BECAUSE you are loved.

Three

Ok, let's talk about some very practical things.

You know how you should eat and exercise. And you know how important it is. Don't punish yourself by acting like it doesn't matter.

Yes. I said, "punish yourself."

Don't punish yourself out of guilt. Don't hurt yourself out of anger. Don't commit slow suicide out of cowardice.

People who are excited about their future and think they have something important to accomplish in the world tend to take care of themselves and their bodies. They know they have to be around and want to be around.

Where have you gotten off track?

Do you want to be around? Do you believe there are important things for you to do? How long do you really want your body to last? Do you think people will be better off if you are here or if you are gone? Think of specific people in your life. Will they be better off if you are healthy or unhealthy? Hey, think about those who you suspect don't even like you. Would you like them to hear that you are taking care of yourself or letting yourself go?

Think about it.

You need to put some things in writing, a food journal and an exercise journal. Yes, I know you have some very logical sounding reasons why that is impractical or unnecessary. But really, this is important and you know it. Right?

So starting today, you will write down what you eat and the exercise you do. Start easy on the exercise. I've seen your attempts before. Go easy. Think of the long term. And yes, that little snack that you think doesn't matter? It does! Write it down! Drink water! Go to bed on time! All of that matters now because you are finding your path out of this.

You want that, right?

Right?

Do these things. Your body will work better. Your mind will work better. You will feel like you are accomplishing something, finding your way out.

Four

Yes, you have losses,

…people, opportunities, things, places.

There are things you will never get a second shot at. But don't be so sure you know exactly which things those are. You wouldn't want the opportunity to show up and be unprepared because you wrote it off. But you also don't want to keep trying to relive something that you should let go of.

The fuller your life is now, the less those losses will sting. And by sting, I mean wipe you out.

You know the ones.

You know how you get wiped out by wishing it had gone differently, being angry about how it went, punishing yourself or others for how it went.

Make your life full. You don't have to convince yourself that those weren't really losses. They were. Hurt about them when you need to but not every time you can. Because you always can.

Make your life full now.

Five

Everything that goes wrong, every irritation, gets a hotline right to your emotions.

They all feel like great candidates to be the "last straw."

And now this? On top of everything else?!

…Those words that you use as you place it on top of your heap, as you think about the injustice, the irony, the cruelty of "another" thing thrown at you.

Yes, I know about your heap, the pile of "things gone wrong." You didn't make up those things, but you did organize the piles. Listen, don't make piles out of these, not like this. Let each of these things stand alone. Don't make them into a pattern, a trend, a message, a warning, a judgment.

Things will go wrong today, tomorrow. Bad things will happen. When they do, it does not mean what you fear it means, that all is lost, that you are beaten, that you are the punch line of some ontological joke. If you want to gather things into piles, do it with good things.

Every time something even mildly pleasant happens, put it together with all the other good things you can think of. Build a towering pile that you cannot ignore. Let piles like that form the skyline of your life.

Six

I know you are tired.

A simple task can seem like an ordeal. Remember what I told you about sleeping and eating and exercise? That will help some. But you still will have times as you move through this when you do not feel like doing anything.

This is depression, anhedonia.

Things have lost their inherent pleasure. Only the effort remains.

Going "through the motions" is ok to do. Do not discount it.

Seven

I know that you look at the future and see obstacle after obstacle.

I know you look at the past and see failure after failure. You're right. If success was easy everyone would be doing it. I can't promise you that you will not stumble at one of those obstacles but you can promise yourself that it won't stop you.

Yes, mountains are high and steep, which is why people climb them!

Eight

So how are you?

Was I right about the eating and sleeping and exercising? Are you working on that?

You shouldn't have to wait long for that to help. I mean it works quicker than any antidepressant. Water, good food, activity... I don't have to quote sources or studies for you. You know these things help.

This is not a day that doesn't count.

Today you are moving further from the heart of that dark country you have lived in far too long. Do everything you can to help with the journey. It all counts. Even a day when you stumble and fall, you can make progress if you get back up that day and take some steps.

Nine

There are things you can imagine being different.

That's one of the things that sets us apart from the lower animals in creation. We can imagine.

It's a blessing and a curse.

You can imagine if-only's, what could have been. It's an almost unlimited resource for emotional pain. Don't turn that weapon on yourself. Use it to help yourself. Imagine what can still be, based on what you can do today. Paint that picture, an almost unlimited resource for hope.

Do you really believe God gave us imagination so we could torture ourselves? Imagine what things could be like a month from now if you stay on this journey. What could it be like a year from now?

Imagine good things.

Ten

You have people who believe in you.

True, some have misunderstood you, even hurt you. But you have people who believe in you. What do they see? What is the picture they have of you? I know you have your own picture of yourself but my guess is that the injuries have distorted that a bit, maybe even a lot.

Ok, it's not just a guess.

I know that fear and discouragement over time warp the way we see ourselves. That picture you have of yourself, the one that makes you lose heart? It's wrong, twisted, out of proportion. Borrow someone else's for a while. At least look at it. Don't be overconfident in your own ability to accurately see yourself because lately you have been mistaken...

…and it's hurting you.

There are plenty of legitimate reasons for pain in the world. Your blurred and smudged self-image is not one of them. Turn your eyes away from it for a while.

Trust the opinion of people that believe in you.

Eleven

There are some things, people, places, tasks, that you are avoiding.

I want to be honest with you. This avoidance will be hard to overcome. I will talk to you about it as many times as I need to, because I know it's hard. It's hard because when you avoid something, the "danger" or discomfort that you avoid can be as large as you can imagine. There are no natural limits on it.

The monster under the bed can be as scary as any picture you can imagine. But if you look under the bed it can only be as scary as it is, always less than your worst picture, and sometimes nonexistent. You have almost never found a monster under your bed once you made yourself look.

But unfortunately every single time you didn't look, you felt the relief of not having to look a monster in the eyes. That's not the only thing you felt but it's been enough to keep avoidance alive and well.

So I understand.

It's hard to stop avoiding. I will be asking you though to please be willing to risk more, willing to hurt for a good cause…

…you.

Right now you may not have it in you, but it's coming.

Twelve

Corners. Remember those?

Life has corners you can't see around. Think of one of the times in your life when something good, very good, happened and you didn't even see it coming. It was around the corner and you didn't even suspect it. In fact you didn't even know there was a corner ahead.

There are more ahead.

You may not see the corners and you certainly don't see the good things around the other side. But that didn't stop that good thing from coming into your life before. I guarantee you there is a corner up ahead. Don't be so overconfident that there is no good thing around the next corner.

Remember your limitations in telling the future. And remember how caught off guard you were before by not expecting something good.

Be ready this time.

Thirteen

It would be good if your everyday experiences came with "like" buttons.

You could tap "like" and keep track. They can slide by us otherwise. You had some lately. They may not pop up as easily as if they had like buttons but you can remember some if you take a minute. You need to take a minute more often. So many slip by. Your "unlike" button is working fine though, right? You can pull them up in one click!

Pretend you have a "like" button. Wear it out. Be ridiculously indiscriminate in your use of it.

It's ok.

Fourteen

Here's you…

"Right! I'll just tell myself things I already know and bam! I'll feel better. How stupid! How embarrassing! Good thing nobody knows I'm trying this!"

Here's me...

A little impatient, huh? Mad at yourself for not snapping out of this faster? I know. But I'm not letting you out of this. You want to feel something about yourself? Ok. Try this. Be mad that you ALMOST gave up and then be really happy that you didn't!

I believe in you! Keep going. It will take longer than you want but not as long as you're afraid it will. And the time you have spent reminding yourself of these things? Not a moment of it has been wasted.

Um, the time you spent thinking the things in quotes after "here's you"... Yeah, that was totally wasted time, though.

Don't do that.

Fifteen

Remember what I said about going through the motions?

That still bothers you sometimes. You wonder if people know that you really would rather not be doing what you are doing. You are doing good things but it doesn't feel like it comes from your heart. You feel bad about that.

Let me tell you a story that I don't think happened but might help anyway. People were watching a man try to carry a cross up a hill to be crucified. They stayed and watched as he died. Most people were silent and confused by what it meant. Years later, one of the spectators heard a group of people talking about what a great act of sacrifice the crucified man had made. The spectator felt it was his duty to point out that he had not just watched the man die but had seen him in a garden earlier, praying to avoid this sacrifice, if God willed it.

Now, what if the spectator decided that this man's heart wasn't in it, that it couldn't be such a great thing if there was a struggle so much in his heart to accept it?

Is that what you accuse yourself of when you are "just going through the motions?"

Good things are done by people with internal turmoil.

Sixteen

When we go through hard times we stop doing things we used to enjoy, hobbies, past-times.

There is that one thing that you do. Or did? You like to do it but haven't for a long time. I think you will admit that you have some talent when it comes to that. No, I won't ask you to believe you are the greatest, or even noteworthy, but you don't stink at it. You should try again.

Just try a little.

I know you don't feel like it. I know the enjoyment doesn't seem to be ready to gush out. But try it, a little. The worst that could happen is that you will find no enjoyment.

And you may be tempted to take that as evidence that you will never get better. But we'll talk about that. At some point, sooner than you may suspect, you will find some enjoyment in that activity again.

I will try to resist saying "I told you so" when that happens.

Seventeen

You get mad at people.

You get mad at God. You get mad at yourself. You know what anger is for. It's wired into us so that we have the strength to protect something valuable when it's under attack. Of course in your daily life, not many people are running around with weapons about to hurt people or things, so anger responds to more subtle cues. These can be a look, a word, a pattern of things, something not happening that should happen.

But, you also know that there is real evil, danger, and horror in the world, even in your city. So much of that you can't do anything about, it feels like.

There are things to be angry about.

But you make mistakes with it too. Here are some of the questions that you may answer incorrectly in the anger process.

What is in danger?

How much danger?

Is it important enough to risk hurting someone?

Is it as valuable as I think?

Can I protect it?

Should I protect it?

How can I protect it?

Do I need to do something right now?

Do I need to act quickly or use a more long term strategy?

Try to figure out if you are coming up with the right answers to these questions. All the stakes are raised when you get angry.

There is a lot to lose.

Work on this. Protect people over things. Realize that others get it wrong too. Forgive them. Be grateful for the valuable things you have in your life.

And... You won't win going up against God, by the way.

Eighteen

Be careful of the balance between thinking and doing.

In anxiety and depression, the mind usually takes the biggest hit, meaning that thinking is far outweighing the doing. If I had to guess, I'd say you are spending too much time in your head and not enough time in your body. Of course if you're "doing" involves risky behaviors, angry outburst, or hurting others, you need to reign in the doing and be a little more thoughtful. If important things are not getting done or you can't sleep because your mind is racing, trade in some thinking for more physical activity.

Not rocket science. I know. But I wanted to remind you.

Nineteen

Sometimes the sadness hits so hard your stomach feels like it's been scooped out with a spoon.

You lose heart. You sink inside. Every road is uphill. This is what you feel like. This is not the world changing. It is you changing. The world is still out there like it was before. People are still out there. Opportunities are still out there.

But whatever losses or disappointments you may have experienced step right up to your face and scream to be heard. They make so much noise it's hard to look past them, hard to think of anything else.

Close your eyes and allow yourself to listen to them, feel them for a few seconds.

Now look out of yourself to the world around you, the shadows, the colors, the sounds, smells, textures. Stay in the world around you. The sadness is there fighting to shut out the world but keep looking, listening, smelling, touching.

That was a wave that tried to pull you under. True, you can still feel the tug, but it is ebbing away. Be thankful for the strong beauty of waves, even waves of emotion. Be thankful your head is above water.

Be thankful you have known things of such value that their absence feels like death.

It is not death, just the vacuum left when something treasured is more distant. All good things will survive. They will even survive death.

You have survived this wave and you will survive others.

Twenty

Where have all the people gone?

People and relationships can be a lot of work. Luckily you have some people in your life that are pretty low maintenance. Solid mutually satisfying social interactions are some of the most powerful healing potions out there for you. But even so, when you are so worn and frazzled, almost any interaction can seem like too much work.

At your lowest you shrink from them and conversations die out and you get out of touch. You end up more isolated than you should be. Don't forget you need people and people need you.

Most of the time, even when you have not felt up to social interactions, if you went anyway, you left feeling like it was good, like it helped. Yes, there will be some people and interactions that take more out of you than you get. But the odds are with you.

Don't let yourself get isolated and overall you will be better for it.

Twenty-one

"I can't do this!"

You want out. You want to be done. You want to quit. And you want it to make sense that you would feel that way. It does make sense, whether anyone else gets it or not.

You have been hurt. You have been wounded. You are limping.

You want to not have to walk anymore because you hate the limp so much. You are so angry at the hurt that you want to force it to be gone. Finding a way to quit feels like the closest thing to force that you have. But there is no quitting the pain. It doesn't work that way, by force.

The best use of force is to press forward, through it, past it. That is the place for strength, not in quitting. Instead of "I want to quit the pain." Say "I want to quit being beat by the pain." Instead of quitting the race, pass the runner in front of you. Instead of being broken, break the record. Instead of being left behind, lead people somewhere.

You feel a strength that you do not know how to use, yet long to, so you think of using it to storm out.

Instead of crying in defeat, cry out against the enemy, against the chains, against the walls, that are there to stop you but cannot.

Twenty-two

Hope is believing that there is always another path to where you really need to go.

This doesn't mean you are on the path or that you can see the path. You may not even know what the path is but you believe it's there. I know you have lost a path before. You were on it and could see where you were heading then...

…it ended.

You wonder even now if you are on a real path or just another dead end. Let me reassure you that you will find a path or make one that leads where you need to go. But paths are not made or found by standing still, staring at the obstacle in front of you, no matter how big and impenetrable the obstacle seems.

You will go over it, around it, or through it if you just keep moving.

Twenty-three

Inside you are curled up in pain.

You want to shut out everything and everyone. A medically induced coma sounds good. This screaming pain demands all of your attention and energy. But you've paid enough attention to it for now. It will survive without you watching over it. There are other things in the world, other things in you, that you can turn your attention to.

It feels wrong, I know, to turn from the pain to something else. But it can sit there alone, like a child in a time out. Just let it sit. Don't try to make it stop. Just let it be there, while you turn your eyes elsewhere.

It will scream, "Look at me! Listen to me! I am your whole world!"

That's ok. Let it scream itself out. Let it go on in the background.

You can come back to check on it anytime. You will always know where to find it. It has been less than honest with you and demanded an unfair share of your attention. But you will not reject it or hate it. You will understand that it is pain and pain can be like a fire that devours all that it can, always hungry for more.

It will burnout in time but you will always remember its scorching heat.

Twenty-four

You've come to a dead stop?

Is that how it feels? You have plenty to do. But breaking the inertia, to get moving again, how do you do that? Like a marble rolling across a floor and finding a depression, you have slowed, rocked back a little, settled down into this bowl shaped indentation in your day.

You had been going ok but now every direction is up. You turn and look at the steep angles on every side. No longer asking how you stopped, you wonder how you were ever going. But you were moving.

It reminds me of the mathematician who convinced himself he could never cross the street because first he would have to go halfway, but before that, half that distance, and on and on.

Since there are an infinite number of times you can divide the distance in half, he convinced himself it was impossible because of the infinite number of distances he would encounter.

Enough thinking. Just roll!

Twenty-five

You have stumbled and are still stumbling.

Sometimes courage isn't just for those who are risking their lives doing dangerous things. It is also for those of us who know we have failed, know we have let others down, and yet have to keep showing up, keep going. I know you want to shrink from the world sometimes.

You have been tired for so long.

People have been patient for so long. They have rooted for you, cheered you on, supported you and still you stumble. I know you are too concerned at times about disappointing them. You fear they might feel sorry for you, in a bad sort of way that leads them to write you off. I know. You need them to keep believing in you and are afraid they will stop.

Here is the best thing you can do to fight off that fear. Keep going. They need to see your courage to keep going.

Stumble courageously.

Twenty-six

You may have noticed by now that all is not smooth sailing on this trip.

The graph of progress is not a straight line angling steeply up. It is jagged with peaks and valleys, even lowlands that feel beneath sea level. Do not let this discourage you. Your path is still upwards and your destination is outside of this inhospitable country. Part of you will always be ready to make a judgment on your chances of making it out.

When a sudden gust of gravity comes along, and you crash face first into the pavement, you will feel as though your chances of succeeding have also crashed.

But they haven't.

Your chances of never failing have crashed, but that happened long ago. You don't get to make it though life being a person that has never known failure or set back.

No one ever has an all "upward and onward" journey. If you hear that kind of story, you can be sure it has been edited for TV or some consumer market.

You, on the other hand, are living an unedited story.

Don't be discouraged by the failures and steps backwards. Let those times develop a perseverance and determination. You missed out on an ideal life long ago. There is no such thing. But there is a good life, a meaningful life, even an inspiring life. That is the kind of life available to you.

You'll take that, won't you?

Twenty-seven

I want you to stop what you're doing.

Sit down and really listen to me. Turn off the music. Shut the door. Go in another room. Get away from people, whatever you have to do.

Okay? I have your attention?

I know you feel like there are parts of you that are broken, crushed, can't be put back together. You have lost so much and you are afraid of losing even more. I know that you are hurt more than people know, but I also know that you are stronger than you think you are.

You are not going to give up and I am not going to give up on you.

I know there are times when your heart turns to water and your mind wants to close its eyes to everything and never open them again.

This is more than a wave. It is high tide. You strain your neck to keep your head above water. But you are breathing and you can see shore. You are not going under. You are not going to drown.

At times like this you need to move towards shore even if it is inch by inch. The shoreline will always be there. Your panicked thoughts will tell you otherwise but you can't trust them completely. Turn the volume down on all of your thoughts except the one that says "I will make it to shore." That one thought is all you need at these times.

Your body will keep breathing if you let it.

All it needs to hear is, "I will make it to shore."

Twenty-eight

Memories pop up without a warning and with a will of their own.

This is a trauma reaction. Playback starts where and when it wants to and triggers all the emotions. Places, so many places, words, people, news, conversations, spread out across your day like a mine field. Stepping too near one sets off an explosion of emotions that reverberates through your body.

Maybe it's primary trauma, vicarious trauma, betrayal, moral injury. The terms all overlap instead of staying in their respective boxes but find commonality in the resulting slow burn. You know it has dismantled your sense of safety, your moral infrastructure, your spiritual identity, your ability to trust.

But you have been taking the risk to trust again, holding on tight to whatever you can when it backfires.

You will keep risking because you know the alternative is isolation.

Twenty-nine

Life goes on and there are things to celebrate.

There are birthdays, graduations, weddings. I know celebration feels foreign when you are barely dragging yourself along but you and others need celebration. You need to mark good events. Put on a good face. Don't complain.

Say the words of celebration. "I'm happy for you. Good job. I'm proud of you." You are not lying. You are speaking the truth in spite of your emotional state. Your mind may try to rebel and accuse you of being in denial, being a fake, not being real.

That's ok.

You know the truth that the oppressive hopeless mindset you are stuck in is the imposter, the lie. Celebrate the good things in the lives of others.

You will not regret noticing the good.

Thirty

You look for magic.

I understand why but the basics that you already know are what will get you through this.

Keep going. Take care of your body. Stay connected to people. Let them know you appreciate them. Work hard especially when you want to quit. Trust God to take care of the big things. Let the little things go. Throw your effort at the stuff in between. Hold your head up. Expect good things will be wrapped in every sort of package imaginable.

You know there are people you will always support and love no matter what you see happening in their life. Remember there are people who feel the same way about you. Don't let that bounce off. Soak it in. When you don't know where to start, do something. When you don't know how, ask for help. When you let someone down, apologize and do what you can to minimize the impact, knowing you can never really make up for it. When you realize you are avoiding something, take a step toward it and breathe.

When you drop something, pick it up.

Thirty-one

You slip and fall into a hole.

But then instead of trying to climb out you search for some way to cover the hole with you inside. You crouch down into the darkest corner and soak in the darkness. Stand up. Stick your head out. Breathe the better air. Come with me out of the hole. Bring all of yourself. It takes courage but stand up taller.

Courage is the right approach, not shame.

Trust me. You know I'm right. You do not belong in the hole.

You grow weaker there, not stronger.

Thirty-two

There are days when you don't think you can get out of bed.

Frankly, you don't want to, but then somehow you do. It isn't pleasant. There is no miraculous feeling of "get up and walk." You just bring the pain with you into your day as you go. But you get up. You get moving. You decide then if that was a failure or a success. You are tempted to call it a failure because the depression did not lift. You did not "feel" like getting out of bed.

Don't give into that temptation. You succeeded in getting out of bed, climbing out of the hole instead of sinking deeper. That counts as an achievement, showing up when you really wanted to hide. That counts as courage. Don't discount it. Determine to keep doing it, no matter what.

That task you did at home over the weekend? You get to count that too. It seemed like a mountain but you did it. Yes, it was harder than it would have been if you felt well. It took you a little longer. But you got it done.

Determine to do that more. People in your life need you to do that. I need you to do that.

Thank you.

Thirty-three

Remember what I said about avoidance?

I was right about how hard it will be to conquer, wasn't I? There are things today that you have been putting off because the anxiety it provokes screams, "Run away!" The depression moans, "I'm too tired. I can't do it." The pain says, "I can't concentrate on that right now. I hurt too much." The shame says, "It's too late. I should probably just suffer the consequences I deserve for putting it off."

All similar advice from your emotions is misguided, wrong, damaging to you.

There is a certain logic to the advice but it is based on the premise of no hope, no redemption. There is hope. There is redemption. You don't have to run away. You are tired but you can still do it. Your concentration is adequate, even if it takes longer and is not perfect. It is not your job to punish yourself, and in the process punish others.

Courage! Step into the difficulty with a determination to use what effort you can and I promise it will go better than you fear. I promise you will feel better afterwards than you do right now. I'm not letting up on this.

I promised you I wouldn't give up and I will keep that promise.

Thirty-four

I have given you thousands of words now but I am nowhere near done.

You have been taking steps, sometimes sliding back, but taking steps. You are making a very difficult journey out of the dark country toward a better place. It is still very dark but you have seen a little light. Not enough, not nearly enough, not yet. But there is more. There is a place where the light will warm you and even hurt your eyes. There is a place where darkness is not so thick that it sticks to you like tar. I am going there and bringing you with me. It is a good place to live.

You have been there before even though it strains your memory to picture it and to feel the sunshine. You will get there again, and because you have been in the darkness for so long, the light will be so much more brilliant. You will run into others that do not even seem to notice the light. They have not been in the dark place you have and since they do not know the darkness, they do not really know the light. But you will.

You will.

You will delight in it like few others can. You will stick with me and we will get there and dance in it.

You will help others to dance.

Thirty-five

Remember I told you before to trust the designer and trust the design?

I want to say more about that. Most of the time you believe that God is good. I know there are dark moments when you are tempted to believe otherwise. Those pass. But even believing God is good leaves you wondering what it means for your life right now. Your idea of good is so intertwined with avoiding pain and feeling pleasure. It's true that pleasure is good, just not the highest good.

It hits you again and again that God's idea of good must be very different from yours. So you trust him, but trust him to do what?

Here is my best answer.

You trust him to redeem every part of you that you will let him have, no matter how long that takes. I know you would like a different answer, one that tells you what to expect, how events will go. There may be times when he reveals that to you, maybe. But there are things so much more important than you being able to know the future, what will happen today or tomorrow.

That leaves you feeling less than safe? Yes, safety is also not the highest good. God has in mind the highest good. He has designed you with that in mind. He has given you life with that in mind. He has taken things from you with that in mind.

He will be relentless. He will not let things like danger, pain, or even death, have the final say. So, even when you experience those things, he will not move on without you and leave you behind. He will take you in the midst of danger, pain, and death, and redeem you, move you toward what he knows to be the good because he designed you to be his.

I do not expect you to lose all anxiety by hearing this because that also is not the highest good. I just don't want you to feel anxious about the wrong things, like being unloved, abandoned, of no use.

You are designed to be loved, belong, and be used for good things.

Thirty-six

You still lose heart and stand still.

You grasp for things, things that cannot be held. When the truth of that hits you, you sink inside. You wonder what you can strive for, what you should strive for. You are again wanting to know the future.

You are trying to play only games you know you will win.

Thirty-seven

You are turned inward.

Too much you are living in the world of your thoughts instead of the real world. Think less today. Focus outward.

Thirty-eight

You have now.

You have today, not a hope-for or "maybe" tomorrow. You have right now in your hands. How will you spend it? It's something money can't buy, you know? And no one can take right now from you. Your life is ticking past. You can't save it up. You can only use it, live it.

The lives of everyone you care about are ticking past also.

But you have now.

Thirty-nine

You were worried today, nervous, anxious, unsure, restless, apprehensive.

In those times it feels like your body takes over, giving you no alternative, and your mind is dragged along, helpless. You are mistaken on two counts.

First, there are ways to influence your body through breathing, posture, diet, movement. Second, your body does influence your mind but your mind also influences your body. You are not at the complete mercy of your anxiety.

Both your body and mind are tools you can use to lesson your experience of anxiety. Do not give in to the helplessness which is an illusion. Stand tall. Move freely and confidently. Breathe deeply and slowly. Exercise. Eat and sleep well.

Challenge your irrational fears. Calm your mind by grounding your attention in your senses. Redirect your mind to better thoughts. Accept the flow of transient thoughts.

There are things you can do to fight the anxiety.

Forty

You fear that you have made no progress at all, and even worse that you never will.

What could you do today that would feel like progress to you? Let me ask it this way... What was it about your functioning today that has gotten you so disappointed? Prove to yourself that you can do better. You can do better. You need to prove it to yourself though. What is it today that you can do differently that would register on your radar? Promising yourself can only go so far.

You need to see action.

Forty-one

I know your functioning has taken a hit in multiple areas of your life.

Keep going. Keep attempting to finish. Show everyone around you that you are not going to give up. Your friends need to know that. Your enemies need to know that. Those closest to you need to know it the most. Show them all. In the process you will also show yourself. Leave things in your wake that can be marked Done, Completed, Finished. Not just started, attempted, in progress.

Forty-two

You have those brief moments, or parts of the day, when the sunlight comes through the trees and shines on you.

It feels so good but then the shadows seem so much colder afterward. You almost wish you hadn't felt the sun. It feels like such a cruel joke when it's gone again. But it's not a joke. It's a promise. It's hope and it's your future. There will come a time when you walk all day in that sunlight, when you even wake up to that sunlight.

Meanwhile, in the shadows, maybe even right now, remember the feeling of sunshine and let yourself hope. You will always be better off with hope than without it. If you are angry that the sun has gone away again, let that anger strengthen your legs to take larger and faster steps, steps that carry you further and further from the cold, dark country of night, where it is always winter but never Christmas.

Forty-three

No matter how much of today has gone or how much you have messed it up, the rest of it still counts.

Take a step or two in the time that's left. Determine not to step further backwards. You are in the road. Keep traveling. I know that other things don't stop for you while you try to make this journey. Even new stressors show up. But you are on the road to responding better to them. The new stressor is not a sign that you are failing or should give up. It's just life continuing.

Don't wish for life to stop. Wish to live it better.

Forty-four

You want things to be better today, even pray for things to be better today.

But do you think about things being better next month? Do you pray that things will be better next month?

Everything doesn't have to culminate today.

Remember in drivers training when they taught you to focus further down the road so that you could reduce over-correcting? It's a little like that. Think of what results you would like next month. If you keep working for those, there will come a "today" when it happens. The ups and downs of today won't jar you so much.

Everything does not have to be resolved today.

Stretch your timeline. Expand your drop zone and see what answers drop in. This doesn't mean today is not important, only that you can't look exclusively between your feet while walking and expect to go in a straight line.

Zoom out a little.

Forty-five

You remember things from the past that are no longer in your life.

There are holes left behind. It's true that nothing will come along with the same exact shape as one of those to completely fill a hole. Even if the same thing returns it will not fit in the old hole. Give up on trying to fill them. Fill your life, not those old holes. Those holes will stay to remind you of cherished things. Your job is not to fill them and somehow erase them. Your task is to cherish the things in your life now and the things that are coming.

That is the remedy for the ache of things lost.

You may spend some time walking among the holes, thinking of the things cherished, feeling some of the ache. But don't climb down into a hole and disappear from your own landscape. You know those times you disappear? People around you see the far away look in your eyes. You find yourself staring, not seeing. The present and future stop existing and only the past remains?

Yes, you know those times.

Look back but don't stare. If you need to contemplate the past, set aside a time when you can be by yourself somewhere and write down your thoughts. Writing things down is like the cave explorer tying a rope to himself so he can always get back out. Caves are wonderful but tangled and disorienting, like contemplation. Don't let the contemplation overtake you out of the blue and derail your day.

People need you present. You need your presence.

Forty-six

See how they rise and fall, wax and wane, these emotions?

The text or email you almost sent but decided to wait? The emotion subsided and you saw it differently, didn't you? Remember what I said about anger and all of the questions you try to answer correctly?

Other emotions yell for answers too. Are you going to let her get away with this? Aren't you going to set him straight? How long will you let this go on? Why should you take this? How can she say that? Who does he think he is?

Or these... What's the use? Why should I try? How stupid will I look? Why should anyone listen to me?

These are leading questions and the emotion has stacked the deck, poisoned the well, bought off the jury, stuffed the ballot box, rigged the fight.

Wait until the yelling dies down. It will. Wait until the pain softens. It will. Wait until the panic drains away. It will. Wait until the anger burns out. It will.

Forty-seven

Everywhere you look there are tasks you don't feel up to.

They have fed off your neglect and avoidance. You can't find the energy. How are you doing on eating right, sleeping, and exercise? Your body and mind need those things. Do a little today. Do a little more tomorrow. You are not defeated. It's not over. Next month can be better than this month. Next year can be better than this year. You have time to pull out of this.

Even after what you have lost, you have a lot, and there are still things to gain.

Forty-eight

You want to give up, cut yourself off.

"If I can't have it the way I want it, then I don't want it at all."

You know this is called all-or-nothing thinking. That's what it's called but then there's how it feels. It feels like you are torturing yourself for no good reason. It feels foolish. It feels stupid. And it hurts, and hurts, and hurts. You see two ways out.

Plan A is somehow making it the way you want it to be. Plan B is the eject button. You feel sure that either of those would feel better, be better.

Here's the problem. You don't know that you can make either of those happen according to plan. And even if you did, you don't know that it would feel better or be better. Check the intensity of your emotions. If that intensity is high resist putting all your chips on Plan A or Plan B. Stay the course. Keep going through. Stay steady. Keep the commitment. Get up and move forward. Crawl forward if you have to.

Determine not to escape by chasing some idealistic fantasy or trying to press the untested eject button.

Forty-nine

Fail! Fail! Fail! Again and again!

Please be willing to risk that. Without that willingness you never take steps. You have watched children learning to walk. God knew we needed to learn to walk before we could learn to feel shame. It is an absolute developmental necessity that toddlers have no adult concept of shame. They would never be able to get past all those faltering steps they need to take in order to walk. How many times do they fall? How many steps end in failure? They see others walk but what makes them think they should be able to when they fall again and again? Part of it is an inborn drive to go places in life.

You have that drive still but it can overridden by the screaming voice of shame. You can't do that!

You look stupid! That's just for other people, people who make it! You will never be one of them!

You've heard the screams? Yes. You don't have the luxury of the toddler to not know the shame in failure. That makes your fight harder than learning to walk... unless you can, more and more, see the shame as false, mistaken. Imagine a child feeling like another attempt to walk is useless. How miserably mistaken and how obvious the solution: keep trying!

Please risk failure again and again and again, like a child.

Fifty

Right now stand up tall.

Lift your eyes up. Breathe deeply. Determine to act with purpose and conviction. Confident that all things for you end in redemption, not pain, disgrace, failure, brokenness, aloneness, punishment, guilt. No, your story ends in redemption. How does a person who knows that stand, walk, breath? What is the posture and bearing of a person who really believes that? Could you pick that person out of a crowd?

You are working on becoming that person.

Fifty-one

I have something I want you to do.

Find a skill that you can build over time by spending just a few minutes a day. Drawing, balancing, memorizing, playing scales, juggling, stretching... something everyday consistently. There are endless possibilities. This will help convince you, by experience, that little steps over and over get you places.

Think of this as a symbol, or reflection, or allegory of your progress toward healing. Everyday counts. You will see yourself progress in this allegory. As you make progress in one you make progress in the other, daily in small steps that add up. Pick something that only takes a few minutes. Do it everyday and see yourself move forward.

Prove to yourself that everyday counts.

Fifty-two

What did you like today?

Think through your day. There were moments. Do this. It's important and good for you. Got a few? Ok, pick one and replay it. What did you like about that? What is it about you that allowed it to happen? What is it about you that allows you to like it? How can you set things up so something similar has a good chance of happening again?

Go through these questions with at least one moment from today.

Fifty-three

They pass, those moments when you think you can't do it, think you shouldn't even try.

You will get better and better at believing that they will pass. You will get better and better at believing it's okay to try even though you don't think you should. You get to be a person that makes it through this and comes out the other side. You didn't used to believe that. Sometimes you still don't.

Fifty-four

Discouragement, low on courage.

That's how it feels, right? Courage is not letting real or imagined dangers stop you. Real or imagined. Don't spend too much time trying to figure out which is which because in the end your task is to go forward either way. You may take some hits. You've taken some before. Take them while moving forward, not with your back turned. Take them standing.

Believe it or not you will learn to even take them smiling, knowing you are doing what's right. But smiling or not, take courage. We lose courage, become discouraged, when we convince ourselves that the best thing to do is stop, not go forward.

Doubt that message if you hear it in your head.

Fifty-five

Get back up.

I know it's hard, especially when you stay down so long and bleed so much. It makes a mess and things get stained with blood. Some other things get left on the ground too. And things break. The most important thing is to get back up. The things lost, broken, stained... you can get back to those when you are able.

But get up. Stand. Breathe. Walk.

Fifty-six

The day's not over.

The rest of it still matters. The people you care about and the people that care about you matter. Be there for them, as much as you can, the rest of this day even if you've blown it, even if you failed today, even if you are pretty sure you will fail tomorrow. Fight hard right now. The day is not over.

Your fight is not over.

Fifty-seven

It feels good, doesn't it?

...those moments when you are going forward, feeling some confidence, or at least determination, which is maybe the same thing.

You have gone some long stretches without feeling that at all. But you have had some here and there recently. You will have more. That will become more of your "normal" feeling rather than it being just some aberration, a straying. Think about what that will be like, what you will accomplish!

Your brain chemistry is changing, you know? It's not just meds that alter our neurotransmitter balance and patterns of brain activity. When you spend time repeatedly working on the things you believe, over time you change how your brain works. It is easy for us to accept that trauma will do that, or repeated loss. Don't forget that you have the capacity to change your brain for the better. That's what you have been working on now for weeks.

Keep going.

Fifty-eight

Your vocabulary has had to include "I'm sorry" over and over.

You have that ideal in your head of someone who doesn't need to use those words. You realize that can never be you now. So far all that is true. Here's where the problem comes in. You want to interrupt and say, "What do you mean? The problem is that can never be me!" No, that's not really the problem. No one gets to be that ideal person, although some try to pretend by never saying "I'm sorry." Thankfully that is also not you. You are aware of your faults, the hurt you cause others. The problem is you do not forgive yourself and you feel stained beyond usefulness. You punish yourself and constantly feel in need of more punishment.

You keep waiting for it to come, expecting it to come, and then when that doesn't happen, making it come. Please open the prison cell and let yourself out. There are people and opportunities waiting out here for you. I know it is not as simple as walking through a doorway and this is only one part of your struggle. But it is tripping you up. Keep it in mind.

Fifty-nine

You want things around you to change.

You want to feel like you can change them or at least that "it will all work itself out."

Yes, that would help but you know too much about the world to hang everything on that. Some things don't improve and only get worse. You have no guarantee that specific circumstances will improve. So is the answer despair? That's one answer but is it the right answer?

You also know that to focus solely on the interior life while the world goes to hell is also not the right answer. So here is the answer, satisfying not because it is elegant but because it can play in the real world:

Hope for, and work hard toward, realistic, positive outcomes. Remember you are owed nothing, so resentment is never the proper response to things not working out. The treasures in your heart are a source of joy that can never be taken. Optimism will serve you better over the long run and increase your chances of changing things for the better. This life is not all there is but it is important, and a gift, and sacred. Life is always better than depression wants you to believe. Being hopeful does not mean you are naive. Working hard does not mean you lack faith. Finding inner peace does not mean you have given up on changing the world.

Sixty

Sometimes you just want to run and never look back.

You are sick of feeling powerless to change things. You feel so beaten. You wish the buzzer would sound and the misery of losing could end, the humiliation of stumbling, crashing to the floor, trying to crawl, almost getting up, and then stumbling again...

You can pray for a miracle but don't make the mistake of thinking you deserve it. You have today by the grace and mercy of God.

There are people you care about so much that are hurting and you get so plowed under by your own pain that you feel useless to help. You feel like you are watching them drown. Their pain and yours swirl together and you start to suffocate. Someday you will be able to do more, but today let them know they are loved, and keep going toward what you have to get done. You doing well will help them. I know you are not "well" yet but you are heading there, to a place where you can help them even more.

Keep going.

Sixty-one

The wall of rock rises in front of you, cold, hard, intimidating.

Some would say, "You know you have to climb it." The hard part is you really don't. You can stand here in front of it, even turn your back on it for as long as you want. You just won't get anywhere and you will start to slowly die. Of course, there are no promises for success with climbing the rocks, but you have climbed before, a lot lately. You know that footholds, and handholds, give way sometimes. You have survived nasty falls.

No one can make you climb this and, in fact, the rocks will try to stop you. That's the deal. I can't even tell you that other people have made this climb before, because it's different for everyone.

It will be hard, but my opinion is that it makes sense to try. I hope you do. It is miserable to stand here, undecided.

Sixty-two

That knot in your stomach again!

...the uncertainty, loss, weariness,

...the guilt of not "getting over it" sooner,

...the fear of people finally just giving up on you, because you are down too long.

You know the truth that some people will and some people have. But don't forget the other truth that some have not and some will not. Think of the people you care about, that you would never, never, ever give up on, no matter what. You may get irritated at them, mad at them, confused by them, but give up on them? Never!

There are people who feel that way about you and will show you if you let them. Your fear blinds you to this truth. Then, by not seeing this truth, you find more fear.

Say this, "Some may leave but some will always stay, just like I would stay." Say that as often as you need to, maybe even as often as you can, while you let it sink in.

And this too, think of specific people you care about. Say in your mind, "I will never give up on you. I will always believe in you." One day you may decide to tell them directly. But for now, remind yourself of how much you are still able to care,

…even with that knot in your stomach.

Sixty-three

Sometimes you allow yourself to admit you have made a little progress or have moments when you feel a little better.

The little can seem so little! Does it count? Is it enough? Does it matter? Yes! It's not all that you want or all you will someday achieve but, yes, it matters! Yes, it counts! Don't worry that finding satisfaction in little steps will mean you never see big ones. Don't worry that you, or even others, could easily point out what is still lacking. There will always be room to improve. But, there have not always been these little steps... Remember the long stretches without them!

You want to say, "yes, but..."

I know. I know. It is taking so long! It is still so far! Yes, it has been long and the road still stretches on in front of you. But, you will not get there without the little steps, the little progress. Count them! Cherish them! Collect all you can get!

You will realize one day that they were not as little as you thought, that they played a larger role than you knew.

Sixty-four

You think you have made progress in acceptance,

…taking today as it is given to you, but then... something hits you. A sound, a smell, a memory, a dream, and you realize how much you want something that is not. You think, "How could I possibly have this much desire for something, and accept not having it?" You have a longing unfulfilled, a thirst unquenched.

Acceptance does not merely say, "This is what my life is today and I desire nothing else." Instead acceptance says, "This is what my life is today and over here is my unfulfilled longing. I open my arms to both. I will not demand that one devour the other. They are both true. I will take what good fruit there is from the branches of both trees."

Don't let the day that comes to you scare you or make you lose heart. Do not let the unfulfilled longing scare you or make you lose heart. Remember what I said about not knowing the future? You don't know what will come today, but you know that keeping in the fight today helps to prepare you for another "today" when it comes. You don't know what will come of the longing, but you know what you desire and trying to convince yourself you don't is neither possible nor helpful. It is not true, you know, what some would tell you, that ridding yourself of longing and desire is the path to peace. It is the path to apathy, a very poor substitute for peace. Today is yours and the longing is yours. They both belong in your life.

Let them in.

Sixty-five

You have felt a level of pain that some are unaware of, that some cannot relate to.

It has taught you things you cannot put into words. Maybe some of these things you did not wish to know, but you have learned them nonetheless. Now you find yourself, knowing, among people who do not. A few may, but you are unlikely to know who they are until they reveal themselves. It is a coded signal you each send and receive, you and others who have known intense, prolonged, pain. There is something, similar to comfort, that connecting with them provides.

In many situations though, you will feel alone in your knowledge, in your history of pain. Be careful not to rush to that conclusion too quickly. Others, like you, are careful about revealing themselves. But in those situations, where you are the only one to know, be patient with others who have not, or have not yet, learned the lessons you would have avoided learning if you could.

Be glad for them that they have not had to travel your road, even if it is a gladness that they cannot grasp for themselves.

Sixty-six

Decision making, even a simple decision like what to do next, can be such a challenge that you coast to a halt.

You mull over the options, or try to remember the options, and nothing clicks. Part of this is poor concentration and memory. Prolonged sadness, loss, or disappointment has that effect. But there is something else. Our decisions, no matter how logical we try to be, also draw on our emotions. Logic can only get us so far and then emotion tips the scales one direction or another. If your emotions are burnt out and you are feeling numb, feelings and desires can't provide that needed kick to get you out of a logical dead end.

Logic may push you but emotions have to pull too. So if nothing calls out to you with a promise of enjoyment or satisfaction, you are directionless.

Take heart.

Your emotions, like the tip of your tongue after drinking too-hot hot chocolate, will find feeling again. A major contribution on your part will be to stay out of the way. What I mean is that your emotions are designed to recover from numbness unless there are "complications" that set in.

Fear of the numbness is a complication. Anger at the numbness is a complication. Embarrassment about the numbness is a complication. Hopelessness is a complication. Isolation is a complication.

You are on the road to healing.

The numbness will go away. Your ability to make decisions will improve. For now settle for good-enough decisions, not perfect ones, or impressive ones, just good-enough ones. This may mean you chose the easiest, simplest path that moves you forward, or even sideways, but not backwards. Do not stand still too long trying to make a decision.

Keep moving. Keep going.

Sixty-seven

The moments of sunshine, when all the barriers to light part just enough, and at the right time, to let a ray of light through, are you seeing those?

Are you counting those? They have happened. Some have been very brief. But it happened. The light hit you. You felt the warmth. You could see. You could almost remember.

I saw those times. And I remember the light. Believe me when I tell you it is there. And it is good. You can almost feel it if you let yourself believe me. I know the things you see around you, behind you, the things you think you can see ahead of you... dark places, cold, lonely places, places full of pain. There are places like that, times like that, but they are not exactly that, not exclusively that. Look at them again through my eyes. That dark place has a beam of light that you would see it you can manage to lift your head. That lonely place has people who are wondering how to help. That painful place is a facade of false guilt and shame. The place that feels so cold has a beauty that sparkles.

You are working on improving your vision, your memory. Listen to me when I tell you there are also good things behind you, around you, and in front of you.

I will keep telling you this until you can see them too. I will not stop. I will not give up.

Sixty-eight

I think you are seeing now that there is more to life than these waves of hurt and sadness and fear. More, not less.

You are remembering. There are times when you feel human, like other people, like there is a life you can live. I told you. I knew it. You had forgotten but you were willing to listen, let me believe for you.

All is not right in your world, in your life. But now you realize it doesn't need to be. You would like it to be and, in a sense, it "should" be. But it is not. There was a time when the only solution you could stomach was for everything to be right. But things have not been right in the world for a long time. One of the hardest truths for you to hold on to is that things do not have to be all right for you to feel better. You started grasping at ideals whose time is not yet come. You managed to keep your grip on one truth, that evil is alive in the world. You held that so tightly that it was all you could hold.

You can still hold it. I won't ask you to drop that. You don't need to. But you do need room in your hands to hold other things that are just as true, like the things I have been telling you, reminding you of the things you used to know.

You have begun to know them again. Keep going.

Sixty-nine

You are building on yesterday, today.

And tomorrow you will build on today. And the day after that you will build in tomorrow. Every day counts. You are moving forward, traveling farther, leaving behind the dark places of hopelessness. All is not right in the world. All is not right in your life. All is not right in you. But you are remembering now that you can still live a life you can feel good about. You can still find light and warmth. You can still love and be loved. You can still show courage, compassion, commitment. You can still be creative, helpful, friendly, kind. You can still support, inspire, lead, educate.

You can still be who God made you to be. Keep going.

Seventy

There are things you can change.

I know you have a list of things that you can't seem to change. It's a long list and you keep it close to you. I want to ask you to put that list away for a while. You've been looking at it too much. I think you've memorized it by now. It isn't good for you. It discourages you. And, it keeps you from a more important list. I'm talking about the list of things you can change. There is a list like that, right? Where is it? When did you read it last?

I know what keeps you from reading it, guilt, fear, anger, and more. You feel guilty for not making those changes sooner, fear what will happen if you try and fail, fear what will happen if you succeed. You are angry that you have to make those changes, angry at yourself, angry at others, angry at how long and hard the process of change will be, how long and hard it already has been. I understand. I know what you've been through. I know you have felt so powerless in the face of things that happened to you and those you care about. You wonder why you should even have a list of things you can change, since those things, things so very important, obviously didn't make it on the list. I know how badly you wanted to change those things, stop those things. I understand like no one else does. You carry the guilt of that, the helplessness of that.

I know.

I also know, and am here to remind you, that today is your best chance at making things better. That list of things you can change, do not overlook the power it holds. Please trust me until you can know it for yourself. Today work on that list, give it all the effort you can. That's all. Just what you have to give. Keep doing that and it will be enough.

You will see. You will remember.

Seventy-one

There are many ways to distance yourself from people you love.

You can do it in silence, anger, coldness, carelessness, or distraction. The distance can confuse and hurt. It's hard to tell which is worse. You can be so spent emotionally and physically that you do it without intention. Those who care most about you may be able to shrug it off the first few dozen times, but it will wear away at some part of the relationship. True, this can heal, but I know you don't want to wound people you love.

You have traveled so far.

Take some steps now to renew those closest of connections. Turn your focus away from the turmoil inside and see the people close to you.

It's hard when your wounds and fears are calling out so loudly. I know. But, sometimes you forget this is a battle to be fought. You turn too quickly to the internal voices yelling for attention, without even realizing what you are doing. The auto pilot of self-absorption easily assumes control.

Monitor this today. Remember this battle. It is worth your attention.

It will be good for you and those you love. It will be good steps forward.

Seventy-two

You have come so far and you keep trying day after day, and yet there are still times when you just don't feel like doing anything.

Everything inside you drops and you want to find a dark place to crawl into. This is not proof that you will never make progress, or that you haven't made progress. This is a dip, a slowdown, a faltering step, not a trend, or a warning, or a final judgment. You will have more like this but less than you used to if you keep going. Let this be a reminder of how important this journey is.

There was a time when that sinking feeling seemed like the norm, now it is an aberration, a deviation, an anomaly, something to wade through, not something to live in. You will make it to shore. Keep going.

You will outlast this, like you have before.

Keep Going

There is more to say and some of what I've said still needs to be heard over and over.

I hope you have joined the world again. I hope you feel less alone, less crazy, and more like you belong with us all, traveling together.

Now you will go through life, having experienced hardship, facing the days that come. There are still burdens, right? Some have been placed on you. Some you have picked up on your own.

You know what would be nice? It would be nice if you could hold up your I-went-though-it-already card and get a pass on a few things. I understand why that seems "fair" but it doesn't work. Does it? So, you keep going, counting all the joy that you can, collecting all the pieces of good that you can. Thankfully you are better at that than you used to be.

I am coming to the end of my words here, but you have been getting better at finding your own words, and you may hear from me again. Until then, please keep going.

Copies can be purchased at
167hours.net/thingsIusedtoknow.

I would love to get comments from you about the book. Please give me your feedback by visiting my blog at 167hours.net. Thanks!

- David W Hamilton